The Waterman/Harewood Piano Series

Piano Lessons Book 3

with Fanny Waterman and Marion Harewood

Faber Music Limited

London

© 1973, 1979 by Faber Music Ltd
First published in 1973 by Faber Music Ltd
3 Queen Square London WC1N 3AU
New edition first published in 1979
Cover photograph by Maurice Foxall
Printed in England by Caligraving Ltd

ISBN 0-571-50311-X

The authors would like to thank Benjamin Britten and Faber Music Ltd
for their permission to include in this book *Waltz No. 2* from *Five Waltzes* (1924).

To buy Faber Music publications or to find out about the full range of titles available
please contact your local retailer or Faber Music sales enquiries:
Tel: +44 (0)1279 82 89 82   Fax: +44 (0)1279 82 89 83
sales@fabermusic.com   www.fabermusic.com

Contents

To the pianist

When you have learnt the notes of a piece, you should be aware of fulfilling three rôles during your practice:

1. The Performer—plays a few phrases.
2. The Listener—listens and stops to recall the sounds he or she has produced.
3. The Critic—assesses and analyses the playing (perhaps it was too loud, too soft, too quick, too slow).

This process of performing, listening, criticizing and then repeating until you are satisfied with the results is what practising is all about.

All pianists have a great disadvantage. They cannot carry their own piano with them and often have to play on indifferent instruments. Do not make this an excuse for not playing well. By now you will be developing your own individual tone-quality, phrasing and rhythm, and you should be able to produce *your* sound on any reasonable piano.

To the teacher

In PIANO LESSONS BOOK 3 the young pianist's attention is drawn to the various elements which form a piece of music: to the shape of a melody and a phrase; to the functions of rhythm and harmony; to the many possibilities of dynamics and colour. The aim of this book is to make the pupil more aware of the music itself and to emphasise that technique, however important, is not an end in itself but a means of communicating the composer's ideas.

However, a music tutor has its limitations, because so much depends on the individual pupil's hand, ear and general musical ability. The teacher should collaborate with the pupil on the following points:–

1. **Scales and Arpeggios** Mozart wrote in a letter about one of his pupils that if he were her regular teacher he would 'lock up all her music and make her practise, first with the right hand and then with the left, nothing but scales, trills, mordents and so forth, very slowly at first, until each hand should be properly trained'.

The teacher should discourage the merely mechanical practising of scales and arpeggios; to help give the young pianist a fresh outlook on an old problem an appendix, *Playing with Scales*, will be found at the end of this book. Here are set out over twenty different ways of practising the C major scale, which can be applied to other scales—harmonic and melodic minor, chromatic, etc.—and to arpeggios. The variety of rhythms, tonal colours and other technical approaches will make the pianist aware of the different sounds and musical functions of scales and arpeggios in all music.

It is suggested that from Chapter I teacher and pupil should choose scales in keys relevant to the pieces being studied, which the pupils should write out in a manuscript book with their correct fingering. The same applies to arpeggios after Chapter III; particular attention should be given to the Breaking-up method and to the Thumb exercises. Both scales and arpeggios should always be practised first with hands separate, then slowly together. The speed should then gradually be increased to $\quad = 112$.

2. **Fingering** Although the authors have carefully fingered the music, it is essential that the teacher checks that this fingering is suitable for the pupil's hand, otherwise it must be adapted or 'made to measure'.

3. **Pedalling** Only a few pedal indications have been included. The teacher must use his discretion as to how much (or how little) the pupil is capable of using.

4. **The Metronome** can be useful to set a speed. It strengthens the rhythm and prevents 'running away' in quick passages and 'dragging' in slow (or vice versa!). It will help to maintain the basic pulse throughout the piece, but it must be used with discretion to avoid mechanical playing.

5. **Sight Reading** is such a useful accomplishment that it should not be neglected. The pupil should borrow music from libraries to improve this ability and increase his knowledge of the musical repertory.

6. **Aural Tests** help the pupil to listen more attentively to pitch, rhythm and harmony.

For American readers
The British term 'note' signifies both the written note and the tone it represents. It is used throughout this book in both senses.

CHAPTER ONE
Musical Detective

When a composer writes a piece of music, he gives us not only the notes, but also some clues on how to play them. A good pianist is a good detective, able to spot *all* the clues.

How good a detective are you? Look carefully at the piece below and before you play be sure you have observed all the following:

1. Name of composer and his dates
2. Title of piece
3. Tempo indication
4. Key signature
5. Time signature
6. Dynamics

7. Phrase marks (slurs)
8. Accents (*sf*)
9. Tied notes
10. Rests
11. Repeat marks
12. 1st and 2nd time bars (measures).

It is vital to follow and memorize the composer's markings—you would be committing a 'musical crime' by ignoring them. Apply this method of musical observation and detection to all the pieces you study.

Minuet

Ludwig van BEETHOVEN
(1770-1827)

Here is the same piece again without the clues. Mark them on the music without turning back to the previous page. Remember: composer, title, tempo, key signature, time signature, dynamics, phrase marks, accents, tied notes, rests, repeat marks, 1st and 2nd time bars (measures). Then play the piece again and learn the Trio.

Menuetto da capo

Scales

Scales are not just extended finger exercises; they play an important part in all music. Once you can play a scale evenly, you should practise it at different speeds and with different dynamics. In this way you will become familiar with the types of scale passages you will find in your pieces. You will also improve the mechanism of your fingers so that you will be able to play more beautifully.

1. Breaking up

The last note of each group must be very short. By accenting it you will give the group a sense of direction, and rhythmic impetus.

(a) **Note by note:**

(b) **Beat by beat:**

Here is an illustration of the way in which Beethoven uses fragments of scales at the opening of the last movement of his First Symphony:

2. Turning the corner

Be careful when 'turning the corner' at the top of the scale. Pay special attention to accentuate the beats at the top: this will give you a feeling of security when turning round the corner. Practise hands separately, then together.

Turning the corner

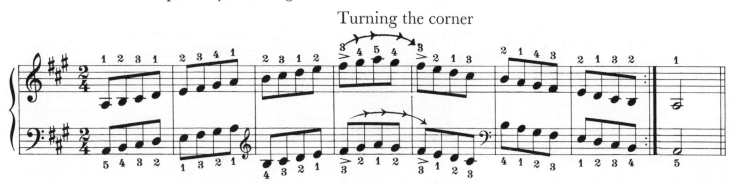

3. Dynamics

Study
from Op. 27

Dimitri KABALEVSKY
(b. 1904)

Allegro vivace

Triplets

When a beat is divided into three equal parts this is called a triplet, indicated by a '3' over the notes.

Notice that three notes grouped as a triplet are equal in value to two ordinary notes of the same kind.

Triplet Exercises

Clap these exercises with a metronome to keep the beat.

Mazurka
from Children's Album Op. 39

Peter Ilyich TCHAIKOVSKY
(1840-1893)

Clap the rhythm of the right hand before you learn the notes.

CHAPTER TWO
Hand Movements

Practise the following movements of the hand away from the piano:

1. *Vertical movement* Move the hand up and down from the wrist, as if waving goodbye.
2. *Rotary movement* Rotate the forearm from the elbow, as if turning a door-knob.
3. *Lateral movement* Rest your hand on the edge of the table with bent fingers in a playing position. Without moving the fingers, move your wrist from side to side.

1. Vertical (Staccato)

Henri BERTINI
(1798-1876)

2. Rotary

When you reach the right-hand fifth finger in bars (measures) 1, 2, 5 and 6, spring off the key, turning the palm of the hand upwards.

Carl CZERNY
(1791-1857)

Carl CZERNY

3. Lateral

Herman BERENS
(1826-1880)

Russian Dance

from Children's Album, Op. 39

Peter Ilyich TCHAIKOVSKY

Allegro

from Sonatina in G

Joseph HAYDN
(1732-1809)

Prelude
from the Wilhelm Friedeman Bach Book

Johann Sebastian BACH
(1685-1750)

*In Bach's day composers wrote very few instructions in their music. You yourself must work out the dynamics, phrasing and speed.

CHAPTER THREE
Melody

To continue your investigations as a musical detective you should now examine the *notes themselves* for further and less obvious clues.

Answer the following questions about this familiar tune, *Lavender's Blue:*

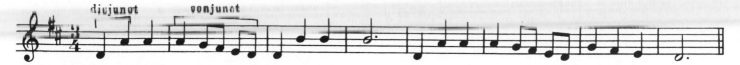

1. Which is the lowest note? Which is the highest note?
2. Where is the largest interval? What is this interval?
3. How many repeated notes are there?
4. Which are the longest notes? Which are the shortest notes?

When a melody progresses in steps, this is called conjunct motion. When it takes a leap up or down, this is called disjunct motion.

First sing and then play the melody above. Stress the larger intervals, so that you feel yourself stretching to reach the top note.

You should always be aware of the shape of a melody: this will help you to understand which notes should be stressed and which can be played with less emphasis. Compare a melody to a sentence in speech—not every word is equally important and only the most meaningful words are emphasised.

German Dance
from Op. 33

Franz Peter SCHUBERT
(1797-1828)

Notice that the melody of this Dance moves conjunctly, whereas that of the following Waltz generally moves disjunctly. At first play only the melodies of the right hand, being fully aware of the conjunct and disjunct intervals (the teacher should play the left-hand part).

Waltz

from Op. 18a

Franz Peter SCHUBERT

Arpeggios

The word arpeggio means the spreading of the notes of a chord, up or down.

C major arpeggio in root position

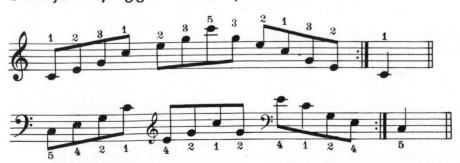

Thumb Exercises for Arpeggios

When putting the thumb under the hand, you must move the wrist slightly outwards (lateral movement) to enable the thumb to reach its note without a break in the sound. Keep the elbow as close to the side of the body as possible.

Two Studies

Carl CZERNY

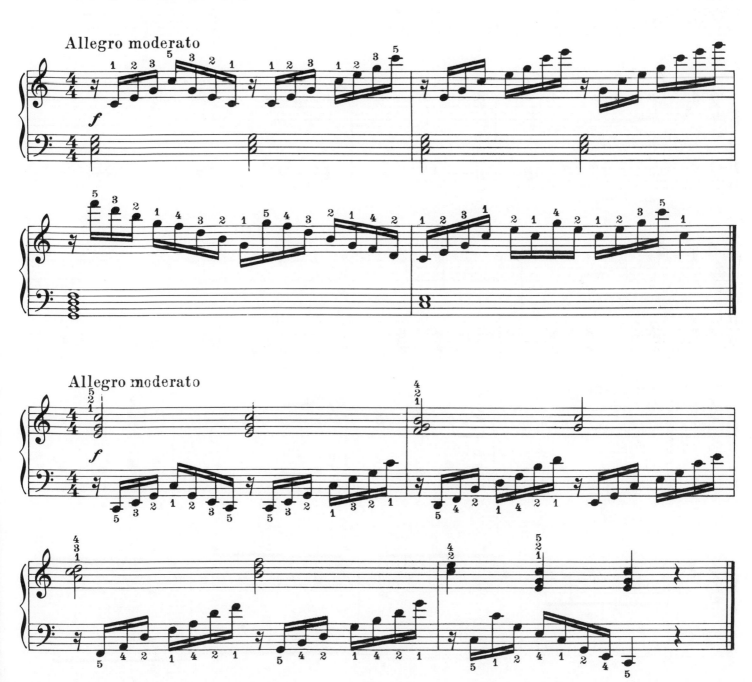

Grandmother's Minuet

Op. 68 No. 2

Edward GRIEG
(1843-1907)

Clowns
Op. 39

Dimitri KABALEVSKY

In this piece it is important to make a point of the disjunct intervals, in order to portray the daring antics of the clowns.

Ornaments

Composers often add ornaments to their melodies, not only to decorate them but also to sustain their flow. In performance all ornaments must be woven into the texture of the music and must never be just patched on.

Turns ∾

Turns can be played in different ways depending on their context and the speed of the music. The following is the most usual rhythm, written out in full to make it clear. Further examples occur below and in the pieces.

Carl CZERNY

An accidental below or above the turn refers to the small (auxiliary) notes.
Play this first as before, then with a different rhythm:

Carl CZERNY

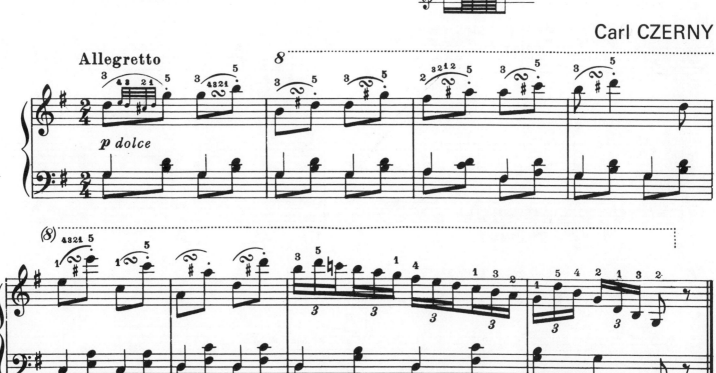

Trills *tr*

Practise 'breaking up' beat by beat, as with scales (page 7).

Carl CZERNY

Trills and Turns

The trill and turn should be played as follows:

Carl CZERNY

Carl CZERNY

Mordents 〰

Allegretto vivo

Carl CZERNY

Grace Notes

Appoggiatura Written  Played

Acciaccatura Written  Played

La Caroline

Carl Philipp Emanuel BACH
(1714-1788)

Le Dodo
French Cradle Song

François COUPERIN
(1668-1733)

(a) ❧ = an inverted mordent.

Musical Clock

Joseph HAYDN

CHAPTER FIVE

Making the Piano Sing

Since the piano is a percussive instrument, i.e. the hammers hit the strings and bounce back, all pianists have the problem of learning how to make the piano sing. Here are three ways to help you to cultivate a sustained singing tone-quality:

1. Intentional overlapping of notes in a melody.
2. Balance of tone between melody and accompaniment.
3. Use of the sustaining pedal.

Overlapping

Play the opening bars of *A Toye* as written out below with special attention to the tied notes. Slightly flatten your fingers to produce a beautiful singing tone-quality.
Listen to the overlapping notes at the pause:

A Toye

Giles FARNABY
(c. 1560-1600)

Use the overlapping technique as often as possible throughout the piece. Suggestions for over-lapping are marked with an O.

Andante

Balance

The speed and weight with which you strike the key determines the volume of sound. You must learn to strike the key at many different speeds from very slow *(pp)* to very fast *(ff)* to give you a wide range of dynamics. In the *Cradle Song* apply this to balance the main right-hand melody against the softer triplets.

Stop and listen at the pauses:

Cradle Song
from Twenty Piano Pieces, Op. 124

Robert SCHUMANN
(1810-1856)

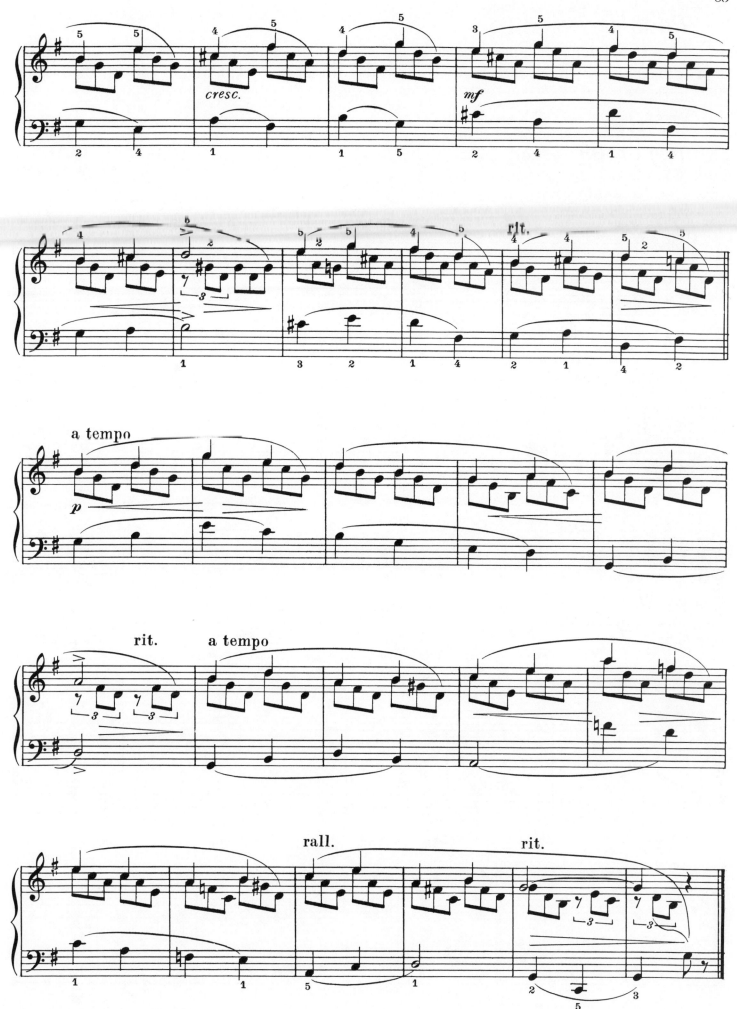

Pedal

Balance the right-hand melody against the left-hand accompaniment. Use the sustaining pedal to help you to enrich the sound. Also use the overlapping technique to connect the disjunct intervals.

Waltz
from Op. 39

Johannes BRAHMS
(1833-1897)

CHAPTER SIX
Chords

Chords provide the harmony to a piece of music. With melody and rhythm, harmony is one of the most important elements in music, helping to give a sense of direction and to create mood and atmosphere.

Chord Practice

The notes of each chord must be struck simultaneously, and released absolutely together. This will avoid a 'wobbly' sound.

Carl CZERNY

Balance of notes in chords

Very often the top note of a chord is the melody note, and the lower notes fill in the harmony. You must make the melody note sing out by playing it louder and very slightly before the other notes of the chord. To help you achieve this, straighten the finger which plays the melody note, and bend the other fingers. Practise the opening of Tchaikovsky's *Chorus* like this:

Right-hand Balance

Balance between Hands

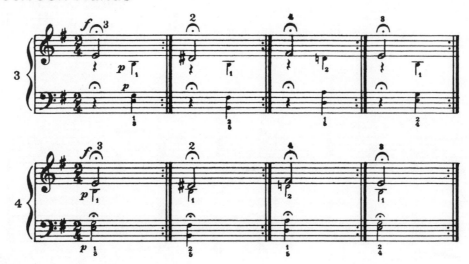

Chorus
from Children's Album, Op. 39

Peter Ilyich **TCHAIKOVSKY**

Imagine that a procession of chanting pilgrims is approaching from afar *(p)*, getting nearer and nearer (<) passing your window *(f)* and gradually disappearing (>) until they are out of sight *(ppp)*. Pay special attention to the pedal, and make sure you change cleanly at each different harmony. Use the soft pedal at the end to help you to get the distant sound of the pilgrims disappearing.

Adagio
from Sonatina in C

Wolfgang Amadeus MOZART
(1756-1791)

Apply the chord balance exercises to this and the following piece.

Country Song
from Album for the Young, Op. 68

Robert SCHUMANN

At a moderate speed
(Im mässigen Tempo)

Courante

George Frederick HANDEL
(1695-1759)

Rhythm

When you play a piece imagine that you are going on a journey in time. You should know your destination, but also be aware of the delights and surprises on the way. It can be a long journey, as in a Beethoven Symphony, or a short journey as in the Bach *Polonaise* in G minor below. You can go slowly, as in Tchaikovsky's *Chorus*, or run quickly as in Handel's *Courante*—but you must always keep on *moving forward*. To help you on this musical journey, be constantly aware of the basic pulse of the piece *and* of the rhythmic patterns into which it is divided. Clap the opening bars of the *Polonaise* against the basic 3/4 pulse.

Polonaise

Carl Philipp Emanuel BACH

Polka
from Children's Album, Op. 39

Peter Ilyich TCHAIKOVSKY

Tempo di Polka

The Thumb

These exercises will help to make the thumb more flexible.

4   Play the arpeggios of C, G and F using your *thumb only*, hands separately.

Study
The Thumb as Soloist

Cornelius GURLITT
(1820-1901)

The Fifth Finger

Play the scales of C, G and D with the fifth finger only, hands separately. Then play the arpeggios of C, G and F also with only the fifth finger. Your playing will not be very accurate at first, but it will improve and help you to get 'fifth finger courage'.

Studies
The Fifth finger as Soloist

Carl CZERNY

The Thumb and Fifth Finger

Here the thumb and the fifth finger are equally important. These broken octaves should be played both *staccato* and *legato*. Practise the left hand 2 octaves lower, first by itself, then with the right hand.

Air de la petite Russie

Op. 107

Ludwig van BEETHOVEN

Thema

Var. 1 *(Balance between hands)*

Var. 2 *(Ornaments)*

Var. 3 *(Metronome to maintain the pulse)*

(Fifth finger courage)

Var. 4 *(Chord balance & speed of key descent)*

(a) straight finger

bent finger

CHAPTER EIGHT
Left Hand Only

Imagine that you have hurt your right hand. Instead of taking a week off from practising the piano, use this opportunity to concentrate on improving your left hand technically and musically. Practise your scales, arpeggios and exercises with the left hand only. Then learn the left hand of the following study and piece.

Study

Carl CZERNY

Move quickly and directly in a straight line close to the keyboard from the bottom B♭ to the B♭ two octaves above. You will then reach your target in good time to make sure of striking the note accurately on the beat.

Apply this to all wide skips up and down.

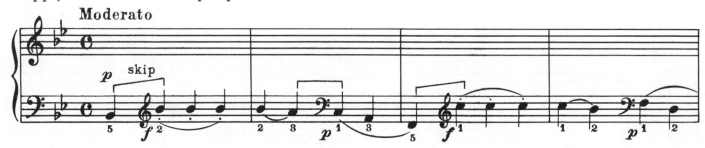

Two-part Invention in F

Johann Sebastian BACH

After a few days play this left-hand part with the right hand, and you will hear that your right hand can still produce a better sound than your left. You must aim from now on to make your left hand as strong as your right hand.

Study

Carl CZERNY

Moderato

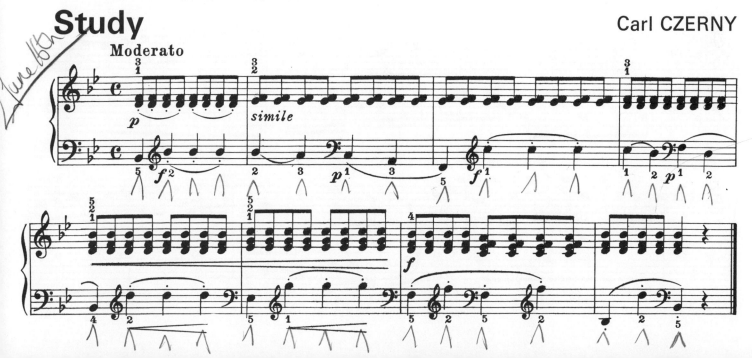

Two-part Invention in F

Johann Sebastian BACH

Arioso con Variazioni

Wilhelm Friedemann BACH
(1710-1784)

Imagine how these *Variations* would sound played by two violins and cello. Play each part separately, and don't neglect the only entry of the 2nd violin in *Variation 2*.

53

Waltz
from Twenty Piano Pieces, Op. 124

Robert SCHUMANN

Lively
(Lebhaft)

(a) Practise the left-hand skips from first to second beats:

(b) Play only the first left-hand note of each bar (measure):

These are the basic notes of each harmony and are related to each other melodically. Imagine them played on the cello.

CHAPTER NINE
Fingers

Co-ordination between hands

These studies must sound as if only one hand were playing. There must be no clumsy joins when one hand takes over from the other.

Remember: *bent fingers—elbows in—low wrists.*

Carl CZERNY

Having Fun
from Op. 27

Dimitri KABALEVSKY

Scale passages

Pay particular attention to the position of your wrists. If they are too high you will have less finger control and produce a thin sound. Experiment by 'playing' a five-finger exercise with your right-hand fingers on the back of your left hand, first with a high wrist, then with a low wrist. Can you feel the firmer touch of the fingers in the second example? Practise the scale passages in the following piece using the 'Breaking Up' technique.

Finale

from Sonata in A, 1773

Joseph HAYDN

Scherzando

Stephen HELLER
(1815-1888)

Con moto

Rondo in G
from Sonatina No. 5

Muzio CLEMENTI
(1752-1832)

Da Capo al Fine

CHAPTER TEN
Phrasing

A phrase in music can be compared to a line in a poem. Read aloud the first verse of 'Daffodils'
by William Wordsworth:

I wander'd lonely as a cloud

That floats on high o'er vale and hills,

When all at once I saw a crowd,

A host, of golden daffodils;

Beside the lake, beneath the trees,

Fluttering and dancing in the breeze.

The words (like notes) must flow, and yet, in order to make sense, the punctuation must be
carefully observed.

Here is a sentence without any punctuation:

'King Charles walked and talked half an hour after his head was cut off.'

Now the same words again with punctuation to separate the phrases:

'King Charles walked and talked. Half an hour after, his head was cut off.'

Music must also make sense. Without proper phrasing, notes make just as much nonsense as the
unpunctuated sentence above.

In the following piece by Chopin commas and other punctuation have been added to suggest the
idea of *musical* punctuation.

Prelude in A
from 24 Preludes, Op. 28

Frederick CHOPIN
(1810-1849)

In Chapter I you saw how vital it is to follow the composer's instructions in order to interpret the music according to his wishes. However, in the Mozart Sonata movement below, the composer has given only a few instructions for performance. So it is for you to decide:

1. The speed of the Allegro so that the semiquavers (sixteenth notes) are even and distinct. Before choosing a tempo, look at the whole piece and particularly at the melody beginning on the second line of page 65.

2. The dynamics and expression marks.

3. The phrasing: pencil in phrase marks where you think necessary.

It is also important to understand the shape (or form) of a piece. This movement is written in Sonata form, which comprises three sections:

| 1. Exposition: first subject second subject | 2. Development | 3. Recapitulation |

Can you recognise these sections?

First movement
from Sonata in C (K545)

Wolfgang Amadeus MOZART

Waltz No. 2

from Five Walztes, 1924

Benjamin BRITTEN
(1913-1976)

APPENDIX
Playing with Scales

Scale of C Major

1   Short Cut to learning fingering

2   Thumb Exercises

3 Breaking Up

(i) **Note by note:**

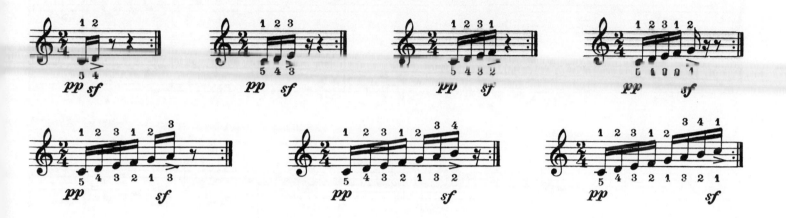

(ii) **Beat by beat:**

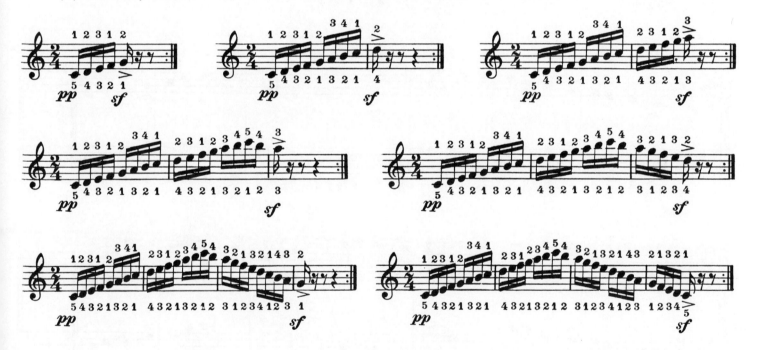

4 Turning the Corner

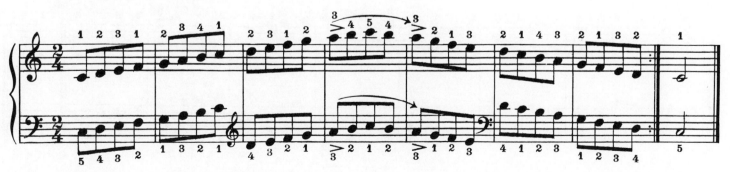

5 Rhythms

6 Tonal Colouring

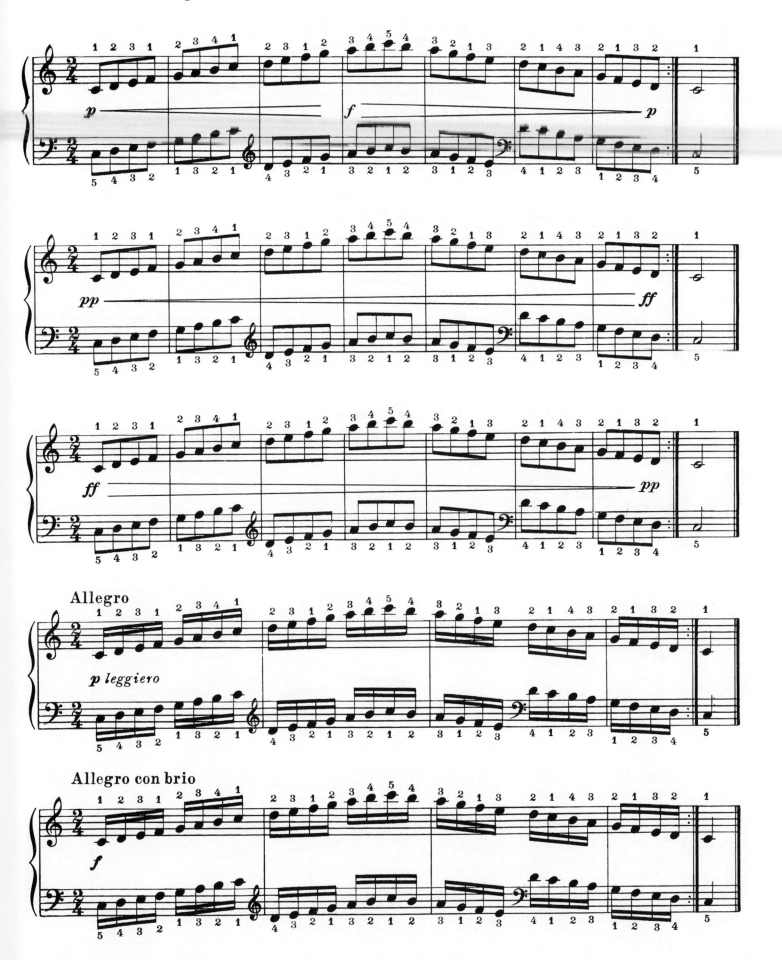

7 Staccato and Legato

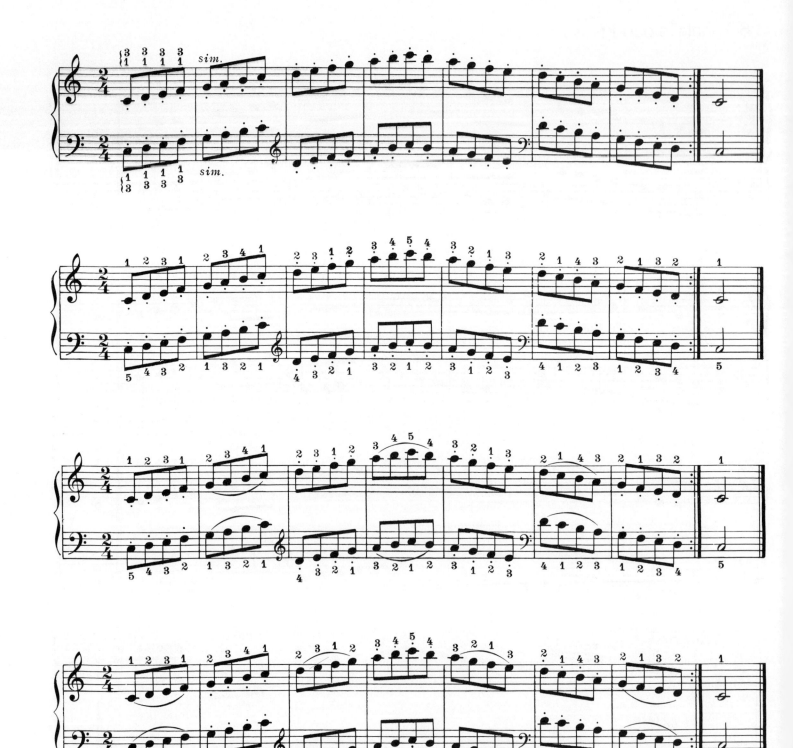

8 Crossed Hands – left hand over right hand

9 Contrary Motion

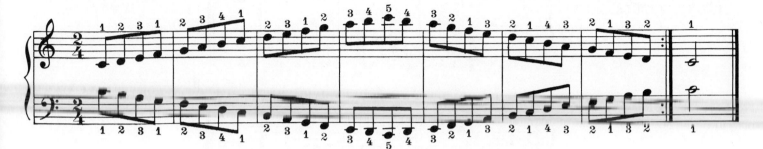

Relative minor·Harmonic

Relative minor·Melodic

Chromatic

Arpeggios

Major root position

First inversion

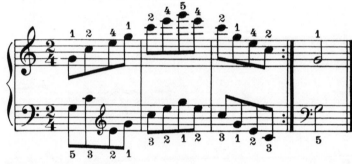

Second inversion

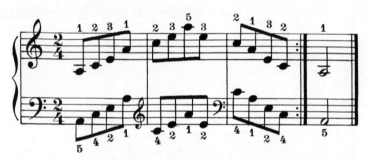

Relative minor
root position

First inversion

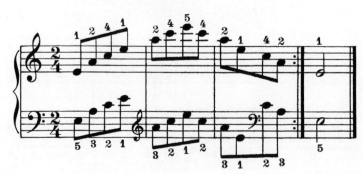

Second inversion

Educational publications from Faber Music

PIANO

Up-Grade! Piano Grades 0-1 *Pamela Wedgwood*

ISBN 0-571-51737-4

More Up-Grade! Piano Grades 0-1 *Pamela Wedgwood*

ISBN 0-571-51956-3

Up-Grade! Piano Grades 1-2 *Pamela Wedgwood*

ISBN 0-571-51560-6

Up-Grade! Piano Grades 2-3 *Pamela Wedgwood*

ISBN 0-571-51561-4

Up-Grade! Piano Grades 3-4 *Pamela Wedgwood*

ISBN 0-571-51775-7

Up-Grade! Piano Grades 4-5 *Pamela Wedgwood*

ISBN 0-571-51776-5

The Jazz Piano Master *John Kember*

ISBN 0-571-51791-9

Progressive Jazz Studies. Level 1 *John Kember*

ISBN 0-571-51582-7

Progressive Jazz Studies. Level 2 *John Kember*

ISBN 0-571-51583-5